WASTE AND RECYCLING

Fiona Macdonald

FRANKLIN WATTS

LONDON•SYDNEY

First published in 2007 by Franklin Watts
338 Euston Road, London NW1 3BH

Franklin Watts Australia
Level 17/207 Kent Street
Sydney NSW 2000

Copyright © Franklin Watts 2007

Editor: Julia Bird
Designer: Thomas Keenes
Picture researcher: Sarah Smithies

Picture credits:
Adam Jones/Getty Images: 29; Ashley
Cooper/Corbis: 13; Bavaria/Getty Images:
19; David Hoffman Photo Library/Alamy:
26; Ian Harwood/Ecoscene/Corbis: 9;
Louie Psihoyos/Corbis: 8; Martyn
Goddard/Corbis: 4; Nation
Wong/zefa/Corbis 16; Niall Benvie/Corbis:
cover, 21; Nick Dunmur/Alamy: 14;
Paul Ferraby/Ecoscene: 22;
Paul Thompson/Corbis: 2-3, 25;
Popperfoto/Alamy: 10-11; Rex Features:
27; Richard Young/Rex Features: 17;
Stan Kujawa/Alamy: 15; Steffen
Schmidt/Keystone/Corbis: 25;
The Advertising Archive: 6; The
Photolibrary Wales/Alamy: 20.

Every attempt has been made to clear
copyright. Should there be any
inadvertent omission please
apply to the Publishers for rectification.

A CIP catalogue record for this book
is available from the British Library

ISBN: 978 0 7496 7602 5

Dewey Classification: 363.72'82'0941

Printed in China

Franklin Watts is a division of
Hachette Children's Books,
an Hachette Livre UK company.

CONTENTS

WHAT IS WASTE?

Waste is everything that we throw away. Almost all our actions, at home, at work, at school and in our leisure time, create waste of some kind. Waste is not pretty, funny or glamorous – but it is worth thinking about, for all our futures.

A load of rubbish!

Britain produces around 300–400 million tonnes of waste every year. This is far more than most other European nations. Today, Britain is facing a waste crisis. Unless its citizens – and its government – take urgent action, the situation is likely to get out of control.

Household waste

On average, each British home throws away 25kg of waste each week, resulting in a total of 30 million tonnes of household waste a year. Household waste contains long-lasting materials, such as glass and plastic, plus food scraps and garden trimmings that rot and give off gases that contribute to global warming. This kind of waste also attracts disease-carrying rats and flies close to people's homes.

Business and industry

Many other kinds of waste are produced in Britain. Around 190 million tonnes each year come from shops, supermarkets, offices, factories, building sites and hospitals. This varied waste includes paints, packaging, scrap metal, wood, rubble and old computers. A further 120 million tonnes is produced annually on farms and in mines and quarries, or is dredged (scooped up) from rivers and canals. It can contain old fencing, worn tyres, dirty oil, plastic sacks, pesticides and manure.

JUST THE FACTS
Every year, the average British household throws away:
● 350 glass bottles and jars – almost one a day;
● 420kg of food and plant waste – over 1kg a day;
● A quarter of a tonne of card and paper – almost 1kg a day.

► The average annual waste generated by a typical British family.

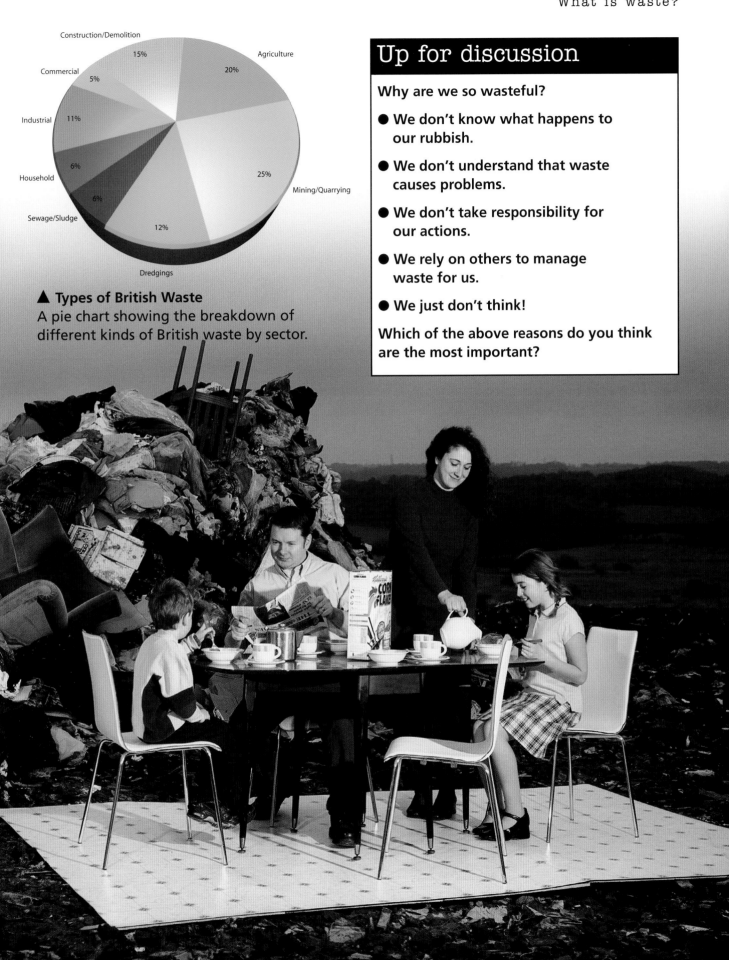

▲ Types of British Waste
A pie chart showing the breakdown of
different kinds of British waste by sector.

Construction/Demolition 15%
Agriculture 20%
Commercial 5%
Industrial 11%
Household 6%
Sewage/Sludge 6%
Mining/Quarrying 25%
Dredgings 12%

Up for discussion

Why are we so wasteful?

● We don't know what happens to
  our rubbish.

● We don't understand that waste
  causes problems.

● We don't take responsibility for
  our actions.

● We rely on others to manage
  waste for us.

● We just don't think!

**Which of the above reasons do you think
are the most important?**

THROWAWAY SOCIETY

Today, we produce more waste than ever before. Modern waste also contains new materials, such as plastics, that are more difficult to dispose of and take a long time to break down (biodegrade).

'Make-do and mend'

In the past, British people did not like to throw things away. Compared with today, most families were materially poor. They had few possessions, and looked after them carefully. If their clothes, shoes, furnishings or tools were damaged, they mended them and went on using them. If objects could not be repaired, they were recycled. Worn-out clothes were cut up to use as cleaning rags; scrap paper was used as wipes in toilets.

JUST THE FACTS

- The amount of household waste is increasing by about 3.5 per cent each year. In 15 years (from 1995–2010) it will have doubled.

- We now use 20 times more plastic than people did 50 years ago.

- We throw away up to 500,000 tonnes of white goods (refrigerators, microwaves etc) every year. Only 32 per cent of these appliances are recycled.

- Every year, 17.5 billion plastic bags are given away in Britain. That is 290 for every man, woman and child.

◀ A magazine advertisement published during World War Two (1939–1945), encouraging people not to waste scarce resources, such as fabric for clothing.

Consumer lifestyle

Life is different in the 21st century. Modern possessions are not designed to last. It is cheaper and easier to buy new goods than to repair old ones. Shopping is now a favourite way of spending leisure time. Advertisements, special offers and eye-catching displays encourage everyone to buy more. People purchase the latest products to boost their confidence, impress their friends and display their wealth or style. Then they simply throw their old things away.

Council tax and rates

Who pays for the growing amount of waste that Britons produce today? We do! Householders pay for it through council

CASE STUDY
Disposable nappies

- Until the 1960s, most British babies wore reusable cloth nappies. Today, most babies wear disposable nappies made of absorbent fibres bonded to plastic. These are used once, then thrown away.

- Disposable nappies are convenient, but they create an enormous amount of waste – a staggering half a million tonnes per year! Used disposable nappies make up around two per cent of all British household waste. Scientists estimate that each one takes between 200 and 500 years to completely biodegrade (rot away).

- New, 'green', nappies, made of washable cloth and recycled fibres, are now available. Besides being far more environmentally friendly, they are also much cheaper than disposable nappies – one green nappy can be reused over and over again. However, many British mothers have not yet been persuaded to use them. Some say that washing and drying reusable nappies uses too much energy. They argue that waste from disposable nappies causes less global warming.

tax, which is a tax based on the size of a property and the number of its occupants. People living on their own are entitled to 25 per cent discount on their property's council tax. Factories, shops and offices pay for waste disposal through rates, which are local business taxes. Many companies also have to pay private contractors to handle their bulky, dirty or dangerous waste. This cost is usually passed on to consumers.

WHAT HAPPENS TO WASTE?

▲ Trucks dumping waste at one of Britain's 2,000 licensed landfill sites.

Around 60 per cent of all British waste is buried in landfill sites. Once rubbish is buried, it is easy to ignore. But the problem of waste does not go away.

Prehistoric

Landfill is an outdated form of waste disposal – even prehistoric cave people dug waste pits. Landfill is also very inefficient. Some buried waste rots, but much of it survives and a few substances never decay. Plastics, wood and metal may take centuries to break down; glass can survive for over 3,000 years.

Waste of space

In the past, landfill waste was tipped into holes and spread with earth. This was called 'cut and cover'. Today, landfill waste is sorted, crushed by machines, then packed into 'cells' lined with plastic. By law, cells are fitted with drains or flues (chimneys), to carry away pollution. Even so, landfill devastates a large amount of ground – around a million cubic metres

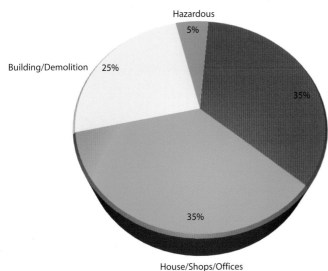

Hazardous 5%

Building/Demolition 25%

35% Factories/Industry

35%

House/Shops/Offices

◀ **Landfill Waste Origins**
The contents of a sample landfill site.

Burning, storing, dumping

Around 40 per cent of British waste is not not sent for landfill. Instead, it is burned, chemically processed or stored in sealed containers. A small, but increasing amount is recycled. Until the 1990s, waste was also dumped at sea or sent abroad for disposal. Both of these practices are now controlled by European Union (EU) rules, but illegal dumping still happens.

per year. By 2010, there will be no suitable landfill sites left in southeast England and only a few elsewhere in Britain.

CASE STUDY
Exporting waste

▼ Dumping waste at sea can cause pollution, spoil beaches, harm fisheries and kill sea creatures. This vessel is returning to a port in Scotland after dumping waste offshore.

In spite of new EU rules, some waste is still sent from more developed countries, such as Britain, to less developed ones for disposal. This is cheaper, and there are fewer controls or safeguards to protect workers. Ships built with carcinogenic (cancer-causing) asbestos have

been sent to India for breaking; old computers have been dumped in Africa. In 2006, Nigerian officials found children scavenging among discarded computers, surrounded by broken glass and poisonous fumes.

WHY WASTE MATTERS

Throwing things away is simply not sustainable. It uses up the Earth's valuable resources, permanently damages the environment, and can have devastating consequences.

Waste is wasteful!

When something is put in a rubbish bin, the energy, raw materials, skills and time used to make it are all lost. So is the value of any fuel that has been used to transport it. By throwing away goods, we waste most of what they contain.

Counting the cost

Replacing old goods with new ones can be expensive. Making new products uses up scarce fuel, natural resources and workers' time, effort and energy. All of these have to be paid for. We would be much better off if we could learn how to

► Thoughtless dumping can have tragic results. On 21 October 1966, a two-million-tonne mountain of coal waste buried the mining village of Aberfan in Wales. It killed 144 people, mainly children.

make the goods that we already have last longer, rather than constantly replacing them with new ones.

Damaging dumping

If waste is poorly handled, it wrecks the environment. Landfill gives off gases that cause global warming and contaminates land and waterways, making them dangerous to use for hundreds of

Up for discussion

How do you think the government can encourage people to repair and reuse goods, rather than just throw them away?

Which is better for the environment – recycling or reusing goods (see p.12–13)?

years. Bonfires – and other uncontrolled burning – release greenhouse gases and toxic fumes. Fly-tipping (illegal dumping) creates eyesores on city streets and in the country. Dumped waste can harm children and animals, who can cut themselves on metal and glass or choke on plastic. Dangerous chemicals from industrial waste, builders' rubbish or old car batteries can leak into the soil and kill wildlife.

JUST THE FACTS

Over six million tonnes of hazardous (dangerous) waste are produced every year in Britain. This includes waste from oil refineries, chemical factories,metalworks, nuclear plants, hospitals, scrapyards and demolition sites, plus household paints, farm chemicals and electrical items. If it is not handled carefully, hazardous waste can cause major pollution. Until 2002, when strict new laws were introduced, most hazardous waste was disposed of as landfill. Today, it is burned, chemically treated or buried at special secure sites.

MANAGING WASTE

To control today's growing waste problem, all waste has to be carefully managed. The European Union governments have agreed guidelines, called the Waste Hierarchy, to organise and control waste management in EU countries. These guidelines aim to get the maximum use from a product while generating the minimum waste.

Reduce, reuse, recover, dispose

The simplest way to manage waste is to not create any. But that is not always possible. Instead, Waste Hierarchy guidelines tell citizens and companies to reduce their waste, reuse it, recover it (for example, by recycling) or dispose of it in a controlled way. Reducing waste is the best option; disposing of it is the worst.

Laws and orders

Waste guidelines can be helpful, but not everyone will obey them. To help enforce the guidelines, the British government has passed laws to control waste disposal. They include the Clean Air Act (1956), the Control of Pollution Act (1974) and the Environmental Protection Act (1990). Disobeying them is a crime. The European Union has also issued strict directives (orders) on waste management. These have been added to the existing British laws on waste.

The polluter pays

The British government tries to limit waste by making people pay for their rubbish. It charges a tax on landfill (£24 per tonne in 2007), payable by businesses and local authorities, and sells licences for disposal of other kinds of waste, such as dangerous chemicals and animal carcasses. It works with city and county councils and with environmental pressure groups to raise awareness of the problems caused by waste. With other leading European nations, the British government fixes targets for future waste management – for example, landfill waste must be reduced to just 35 per cent of its 2001 level by 2020.

▶ Waste (scrap) iron is valuable because it can be used to make a new material – steel.

JUST THE FACTS

- All ways of disposing of waste are now controlled by government laws or local council rules.

- Hazardous waste cannot be transported without a special licence.

- It is a crime to pay someone else to dump your waste illegally.

- New cars must be designed to make recycling their components easy.

- Electrical shops must by law take back goods they have sold and dispose of them safely.

Up for discussion

Which works best to deter dumping?

● laws and punishments

● taxes and licence fees

● information

● guidelines

● persuasion

If you were in government, how would you encourage citizens to produce less waste?

REDUCE AND REUSE

Reducing and reusing waste products are the first two stages in the Waste Hierarchy. They both save valuable energy, natural resources, time and money.

Consumer power

Some of the easiest ways to reduce the amount of waste you produce are free. They include using less packaging and planning purchases carefully. Many goods today, especially food, toys and stationery, are wrapped in wasteful layers of paper, card or plastic. If customers do not like this, they should complain, or buy a product that is packaged more sustainably.

▼ Frozen foods and ready meals often have several layers of packaging.

Choosing wisely

Another way to reduce waste is to choose goods that are energy efficient, such as energy-saving lightbulbs, or those packed in refillable containers. It also helps to buy products, such as cosmetics, that are made without ingredients that pollute the environment when they are disposed of, and to choose household cleaners that biodegrade harmlessly.

Up for discussion

Why do you think so many goods have so much packaging?

In 2007, fashion-conscious women in Britain queued for hours to buy a reusable designer shopping bag made of cloth. Can fashion really help to reduce waste? If so, how?

CASE STUDY
Success in the bag!

In 2005, the government of the Republic of Ireland took action to reduce plastic waste.

It passed a law forcing shops and supermarkets to charge customers about 9p for each new plastic bag that they took to hold their shopping.

In just one year, the number of new plastic bags handed out fell by an amazing 95 per cent.

▼ The tax on plastic bags in Ireland encouraged people to reuse existing bags and baskets on shopping trips.

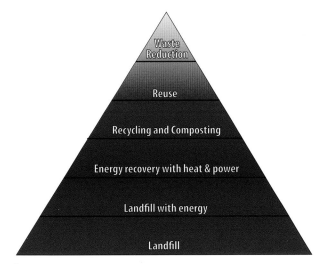

▲ **The Waste Hierarchy Pyramid**
Choices towards the top of the pyramid are best for the environment; choices towards the bottom are worst.

(Pyramid labels, top to bottom: Waste Reduction; Reuse; Recycling and Composting; Energy recovery with heat & power; Landfill with energy; Landfill)

Making an effort

To reuse waste, customers can choose to donate unwanted goods to charity shops or sell them to online auction sites, such as Ebay. They can also choose goods designed to use fewer raw materials, such as rechargeable batteries. Businesses and industries can join government-sponsored organisations such as WRAP (Waste Recovery Action Programme) to share information and training on waste reuse and reduction, learn about new waste disposal laws and develop new waste handling technologies.

RECYCLE!

Recycling means using waste to produce something new. It is part of the third stage in the Waste Hierarchy. The other parts are composting and energy recovery.

Not perfect

Recycling does less to solve Britain's waste problems than reducing or reusing waste. Collecting and processing rubbish requires energy and it costs money to employ waste collectors and workers at recycling facilities. Waste often has to be mixed with new raw materials to make recycled products. Some waste gets lost in recycling – up to ten per cent of most metals. Some kinds of waste decay and become useless. Paper fibres, for example, disintegrate after being recycled six times.

▼ The Impact of Recycling

Material	% of household waste	Energy used	Air pollutants given out	Raw material saved per tonne recycled
Paper	18	28%-70% less	95% less	....
Glass	7	18% less	30% less	1.2
Plastic	7	up to 66% less	....	1.8
Cans (iron)	3	70% less	86% less	2.0
Cans (aluminium)	3	95% less	95% less	4.0

Why bother?

Despite the drawbacks, recycling is a useful way of coping with waste. It gives natural resources a longer life and helps us to get the maximum value from them. It saves fuel and creates less greenhouse gas compared with making new products. For example, recycling two glass bottles saves enough energy to boil water for five cups of tea. Recycling also reduces the amount of ground needed for landfill.

Working together

Recycling can help to strengthen local communities. Everyone can join in recycling schemes. By recycling, citizens learn to take responsibility for their local environment and may start to look at their lives and their surroundings in a new way.

◀ Glass, paper and metals are the easiest kinds of household waste to recycle.

CASE STUDY
From waste to art

Prize-winning British artist Ben Ofili uses recycled materials in his works – including elephant dung! His pictures feature African themes, drawn from his own Nigerian heritage. Ofili says that using elephant waste is a way of including Africa in his work. He also claims that his art 'allows you to laugh about issues that are potentially serious'.

▼ In 1998, artist Chris Ofili won the famous Turner Prize for contemporary art.

HOW RECYCLING HAPPENS

Each city, town and village in Britain now has a legal Waste Collection Authority – usually the city or county council. It is the authority's responsibility to collect and recycle household rubbish, and to control the handling of all other waste.

Collecting

The WCA arranges for most recyclable household rubbish to be picked up from the kerbside in plastic sacks, dustbins or wheelie bins. The rest is taken by householders to official dumps (sometimes called recycling points). The household materials most often collected for recycling are organic waste, such as leftover food and garden trimmings, and paper, metal and glass. Business, industrial and hazardous waste is collected from shops, offices, factories and hospitals by licensed contractors.

Sorting

Once waste has been collected, it is sent to specialised factories called Materials Recycling Facilities. Here, it is sorted by hand, by magnets or by machines. Different materials are forwarded to separate reprocessing plants to be made into new items. Hazardous waste, such as chemicals, paints, oils and batteries, is either treated, placed in a storage pit or incinerated.

New from old

At reprocessing plants, metal is crushed, melted, rolled and pressed to make foil and cans. Glass is melted then poured into moulds to create new bottles and jars. Waste paper is shredded, soaked and pressed to make cheap toilet tissue (a million tonnes a year!), bulk printer paper, and greeting cards. Plastics are heated or broken down by chemical action, then extruded (forced through nozzles) to make a variety of materials, from tough containers to warm duvets and soft fleeces.

CASE STUDY
The problem of plastic

- Plastic is one of the most difficult materials to recycle. There are 50 different kinds. To separate them, plastic waste has to be carefully sorted by hand. Because of this, plastics are not as widely collected for recycling as other materials.

- Plastic is lightweight, and EU recyling targets are set by weight, not by volume. This means that Waste Collection Authorities prefer to collect heavier rubbish, such as glass, to make it easier for them to meet their targets.

JUST THE FACTS

● Don't mix materials for recycling, unless your council asks you to. It takes time and money to separate them.

● Don't drive to the recycling point, if possible. It uses fuel and creates greenhouse gases.

● Don't wash cans and bottles for recycling in fresh hot water, or under a running tape. Reuse old washing-up water to save energy and avoid waste.

▼ A forklift truck stacks bundles of waste paper, ready for recycling.

COMPOSTING

Compost is a dark, crumbly material produced when bacteria, fungi and insects attack organic waste (the remains of living things) in controlled conditions. Composting is part of the third stage in the Waste Hierarchy. It recycles rubbish to make a useful new product.

◀ This woman is putting food scraps and other household waste into a compost bin to make compost.

Left to rot

Around 40 per cent of British household waste is organic. When buried as landfill and left to rot, each tonne produces up to 400 cubic metres of methane gas. This makes up a quarter of Britain's total methane emissions. Methane gas is a greenhouse gas 20 times more powerful than carbon dioxide. Organic waste from farms and factories, such as manure or waste food, produces yet more methane. So do farm animals, as they digest grass.

Top target

Because of methane pollution, organic waste is one of the British government's top concerns. The Department for the Environment, Food and Rural Affairs (DEFRA) encourages local councils and voluntary groups to set up composting schemes. Millions of individual gardeners now have their own compost bins, provided free or at low cost by Waste Collection Authorities. Hundreds of communities have shared compost-making facilities. These provide a place where people without gardens can take organic waste for controlled recycling.

CASE STUDY
Success story

In just ten years, from 1996 to 2005, composting in Britain has increased by almost ten times, from 1 per cent to 9.6 per cent of all household rubbish. In 2005–2006 British compost-makers produced an impressive total of almost 2.5 million tonnes.

'Black gold'

Compost is an excellent fertiliser. It helps plants to grow, improves the soil and discourages weeds. It replaces the need to dig peat (another soil improver) from ecologically sensitive wetlands. Sometimes called 'black gold', compost is prized by gardeners. When sold, it recovers much of the value thrown away in organic waste.

JUST THE FACTS

Earthworms are natural compost makers. Several British companies now sell packs of living worms, plus special containers designed to sit in ordinary household gardens. If regularly fed with waste, these 'wormeries' need no fuel and cause no smells or pollution. They transform 80 per cent of organic rubbish into rich, useful compost.

▼ Earthworms – nature's compost-makers!

ENERGY FROM WASTE

Large amounts of energy are locked up in all kinds of waste. Recovering this energy is the final part of the third stage of the Waste Hierarchy. It also helps to reduce our reliance on dwindling fossil fuels.

Collecting and digesting

Methane gas (see page 21) is collected from landfill sites, and piped to processing plants. It can then be used as fuel in homes and factories. Organic waste from farms, slaughterhouses and food factories is 'digested' (rotted) in huge, sealed containers to make biogas – a fuel that can be used for cooking and heating. Digesting waste is much more efficient than landfill gas collection, and recovers twice as much energy.

▲ Cattle waste products. When collected and processed, they become a useful source of biogas.

heating, or to generate electricity. Any ash left over can be used as an alternative for cement. Up to nine per cent of household rubbish and five per cent of waste from business and industry is incinerated.

Good or bad?

All of these processes work well, but they can be controversial. They cost money, take up space, and use energy. If they are not run properly, they can cause air pollution. Even so, they make use of materials that cannot

Pelletising and burning

Waste paper and plastics can be heated, shaped into pellets, then burned in special furnaces as fuel. Household, factory and construction waste are all incinerated (burned at very high temperatures), along with hazardous waste – from hospitals, for example. The heat kills germs and breaks down poisonous chemicals. The energy produced by big incinerators is used for

JUST THE FACTS

Incinerating waste:

● produces seven megawatts of power for every 100,000 tonnes burned.

● reduces the weight of waste burned by 75 per cent.

● reduces the volume of waste burned by 90 per cent.

Up for discussion

In Europe, waste incinerators have been used for years to provide community heat services for groups of houses and apartments. Why do you think Britain has not done the same?

CASE STUDY
Too close for comfort?

Very big incinerators (sometimes called Energy From Waste Plants) are more popular in Europe than in Britain. At present, there are only 13 in Britain. Plans for more have been opposed by environmental pressure groups and local protesters. For example, in 2006 plans to build a new incinerator close to the historic town of Wells in Somerset were delayed by fears that air pollution would damage ancient buildings and harm citizens. Protesters called for the incinerator to be sited further away from the town.

easily be recycled. They cut greenhouse gas emissions and help reduce waste sent for landfill. They produce fuel for industry, power for homes, and useful residue (left-overs). Unlike present-day power stations that rely on scarce fossil fuels, waste incinerators have an ever-increasing source of fuel – our rubbish!

▼ **How a Waste Incinerator Works**

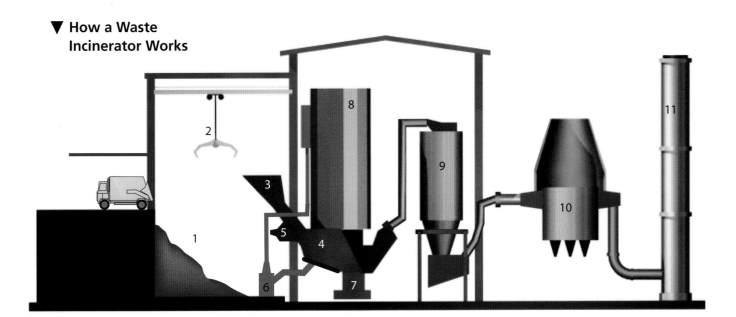

The waste is tipped into a holding area (1) where it is picked up by cranes (2) and pushed gradually into the incinerator (3), which runs at a temperature of 750 degrees Celsius. Heat from the burning waste is used in a boiler (4) and steam from this is piped to a turbine generator to create electricity. The boiler is fed by air from the holding chamber (6). The heaviest ash falls into a collection point (5), where it is cooled by a fan (7) and scanned with an electromagnet to extract metal for recycling. Flue gases containing fine ash pass through a scrubber reactor (9) to treat acid pollutants and dioxins. The gases then go through the bag house filter (10), where fine particles are removed. Finally, the cleaned gases are released through the chimney stack (11).

WHY DON'T WE RECYCLE MORE?

In 2004–5, only 27 per cent of British household rubbish was recycled, plus around 45 per cent of waste from business and industry. Why are we not recycling more?

Slow to act

Compared with other leading European nations, the British government has been slow to encourage citizens to reuse and recover waste. Legal targets for recycling household waste were not set until 1999. Local councils have also failed to provide suitable ways of collecting waste. Arrangements for recycling have often proved controversial, particularly in big cities. About 140 Waste Collection Authorities now collect landfill waste one week, and waste for recycling the next. This system, known as AWC – Alternate Weekly Collection, has led to complaints from residents, who are concerned about pollution from overflowing rubbish bins.

Long distance, high cost

In remote country areas, distances make recycling problematic. It can cost more to transport waste to a recycling point or processing plant than is saved by recycling it, and transport also uses energy. Away from the big cities, rail and motorway links and factories, collecting and sorting waste is expensive. It can be difficult for some recycling facilities to make a profit.

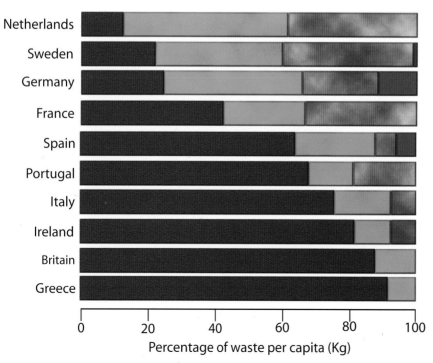

◄ Waste Disposal Methods in Britain and Europe

■ Landfill
■ Recycled/Composted
■ Incineration
■ Other

◀Recycling bins are a familiar sight in Britain's cities, towns and villages. They are often colour coded to show what material goes in which bin.

Unpopular

Recycled goods can be hard to sell. Some consumers dislike them and consider them second best. Others say that they can't afford them – until manufacturers can sell more recycled items, they have to charge high prices to cover their costs. In 2004, a survey found that many citizens did not understand why waste management was so important. They resented being told what to do by the government and campaigners, and could not be bothered to take part in recycling.

CASE STUDY
Mixed materials

Modern packaging often contains several different materials closely bonded together. For example, cartons holding milk or fruit juice are made of card, metal foil and plastic. Mixed together, these three materials are hard to separate by hand or machine, and are almost impossible to recycle. In 2007, only one recycling plant in the whole of Britain could handle them.

JUST THE FACTS

● Playground surfaces made of recycled rubber are softer and safer than earth, grass or asphalt.

● New water filters made of recycled glass perform better than old-style ones made of sand.

● Fleeces made out of recycled plastic bottles are warmer than wool.

● Recycled plastic fence-posts do not pollute the soil, unlike some wooden posts treated with powerful preservatives.

▶ These bright, attractive bags are made from recycled tarpaulins, seatbelts and inner tubes from tyres.

CHANGING THE RULES

Since around 1990, waste management in Britain has started, slowly, to improve. New rules from the European Union have forced the British government to take action on waste and to update British laws.

New directives

European Union directives now control all different kinds of waste, from supermarket packaging to used fuel at nuclear power stations. Even so, it has taken many years for some European rules to become British law. For example, until 2002 around half a million tonnes of plastic, waste oil and tyres were legally dumped or burned each year by British farmers, together with 225,000 tonnes of pesticide waste.

◄ Illegally dumped computers and domestic waste still blight Britain's landscape.

JUST THE FACTS

European Directives on Waste

(The dates in brackets show when these first became active in Britain.)

1975 Directive on Waste (1989)

1991 Directive on Hazardous Waste (2002)

1991 Directive on Batteries and Accumulators (2006)

1994 Directive on Packaging Waste (2008)

1996 Directive on Integrated Pollution Prevention and Control (2000)

1999 Directive on the Landfill of Waste (2002)

2000 Directive on End of Life Vehicles (2006)

2002 Directive on Waste Electrical and Electronic Equipment (2006)

Still under discussion (2007):

   Directive on Construction and Demolition Waste

Revising the targets

Under new British regulations, unlicensed waste dumping or burning is now banned. Landfill is tightly organised and controlled. European Union targets now call for 30 per cent of annual household rubbish to be recycled by 2010, plus at least 50 per cent of all other waste. From 2006–7, it became illegal to just throw away old refrigerators, electrical goods and motor vehicles. A share of the energy or materials they contain has to be recovered or recycled.

Fining the offenders

British Waste Collection Authorities are also starting to impose much stricter controls on waste. Some authorities fit electronic tags to bins to trace and punish anyone who tries to get rid of rubbish illegally. Many local governing bodies plan

◀ New 'spy' wheelie bins, fitted with special microchips, monitor the amount of waste discarded by householders.

to limit the amount that householders can throw away each week, and to charge them for any extra waste. At least one council is thinking about bringing in fines for householders or businesses who fail to recycle a given proportion of their rubbish.

Up for discussion

● **Would you like to have your waste monitored?**

● **Do you think it is fair to fine people for not recycling their waste?**

● **Should people be allowed to produce as much waste as they like, as long as they pay for it?**

A WAY TO GO

In spite of new directives, government guidelines and environmental pressure group campaigns, the average British citizen still throws away around half a tonne of waste every year. That is about seven times the average adult body weight. Britons clearly have not yet solved Britain's waste problem.

Changing hearts and minds

Many people try to reduce, reuse and recycle waste whenever they can. But how can they – and the government – encourage friends and neighbours to be responsible about rubbish? Perhaps fines and charges will persuade people to throw less away? Perhaps people could be paid for making less waste, or for bringing goods for recycling ('Cash for Trash'!)? Or perhaps a prominent TV advertising campaign, led by a fashionable celebrity, might help to win people over?

New technology

Business and industry can also play a big part in reducing Britain's waste problem. Many companies have already made a start. Shops and supermarkets now sell reusable 'bags for life' and are looking at ways of cutting down on unnecessary packaging. Scientists have developed new technologies to recover energy from scrap tyres and to 'crack' (chemically split) plastic packaging to make new plastic items. They have invented furnaces that use plastic instead of coal when making

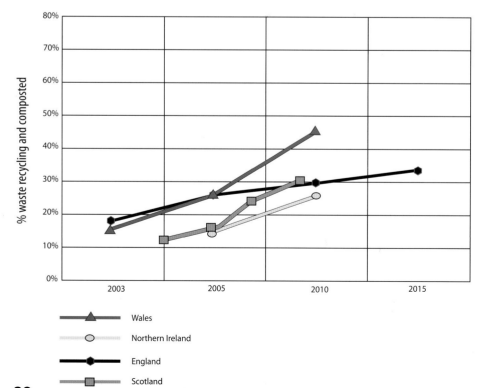

◀ The European Union has set these targets for recycling different kinds of waste.

cast iron, and found ways to ferment (rot) solid waste to create a replacement fuel for petrol. If these new processes make a profit, they might also help to convince people that recycling is worthwhile.

Waste matters!

Waste is all around us. It is not eye-catching, fashionable or convenient – unlike smart packaging, fashionable new clothes, or cheap, throwaway goods. But it does have the power to change our world. For good or ill, waste matters!

▶ Well-managed waste can be useful and productive. This tree seedling is growing in soil protected by chips of recycled rubber.

Up for discussion

The 'paperless office' – an impossible dream?

Ever since computers became widely used about 20 years ago, people have dreamed of a 'paperless office'. But British paper waste keeps on increasing.

● Why do you think this is?

● How can we reduce waste paper levels?

● Could you design an office – or classroom – that functions without paper?

GLOSSARY

Biodegrade Break down naturally after being thrown away.

Council tax Money collected from British households by local councils. It is used to pay for local services, such as waste collection and road repairs.

Cut and cover The simplest form of landfill: digging a hole, filling it with earth, then covering it with earth.

Digested (organic waste) Rotted.

Dioxins Poisonous chemicals, produced when substances like plastic are burned.

Directives Orders or instructions from a central authority, for example the European Union.

Dispose Get rid of; throw away.

Emissions Gases given off by landfill sites, industrial processes or vehicle exhausts.

Energy efficient Designed to use less energy than previous goods or processes.

European Union (EU) A union of 27 European countries with many shared laws and policies, for example on the environment.

Flues Chimneys.

Fly-tipping Illegal dumping of waste.

Global warming An increase in the average temperature on the Earth, linked to the production of greenhouse gases.

Greenhouse gases Airborne chemicals that increase global warming, such as methane or carbon dioxide.

Incinerator A huge furnace where solid waste is burned at very high temperatures under controlled conditions.

Landfill Burying waste in large holes in the ground. Today, the waste is packed into plastic-lined 'cells' to protect the soil, while any fumes are piped off by flues.

Methane A gas used as fuel. It is given off by rotting natural waste and is a powerful greenhouse gas.

Organic waste Natural waste produced by humans and animals.

Pesticides Chemicals that kill insects.

Raw materials Natural materials that have not been processed, such as wood and stone.

Recycle Use waste products, such as glass, paper or metal, to produce something new.

Recycling points Places where waste can be disposed of safely for recycling.

Sustainable Capable of being used sustainably; that is to meet our present needs without preventing future generations from meeting theirs. A sustainable forest, for example, is one where new trees are planted to replace those that have been cut down.

Toxic Poisonous.

Waste Objects or substances that we throw away.

Waste Hierarchy Guidelines to control and organise the safe management of waste: Reduce, Reuse, Recover, Dispose.

FURTHER INFO

Books

Green Files: Waste and Recycling, Steve Parker (Heinemann, 2004)
Sustainable World: Waste, Rob Bowden (Hodder Wayland, 2003)
Earth SOS: Rubbish and Waste, Sally Morgan (Franklin Watts, 2008)
Dealing with Waste: Household Waste, Sally Morgan (Franklin Watts, 2006)
Improving our Environment: Waste and Recycling, Carol Inskipp (Hodder Wayland, 2006)
Sustainable Futures: Waste and Recycling, Sally Morgan (Evans Brothers, 2006)

Information

www.capitalwastefacts.com
London waste information.

www.defra.gov.uk
The British government department in charge of waste management. DEFRA also collects and publishes waste statistics.

www.ehsni.gov.uk
Northern Ireland Environment and Heritage Service. It regulates the environment in Northern Ireland and manages Northern Ireland's Waste Management Strategy.

www.environment-agency.gov.uk
The Environment Agency. The government organisation in charge of protecting and improving the environment in England and Wales. Its website has a section on waste.

www.sepa.org.uk
The Scottish Environmental Protection Agency. Scotland's environmental regulator and advisor. Produces the Scottish National Waste Plan and publishes fact sheets for schools.

www.wasteonline.org.uk
WasteOnline – information and advice on waste.

Practical action

www.compost.org.uk
Composting Association – advice on making compost.

groups.www.crn.org.uk
Community Recycling Network – a network of local waste reduction, reuse and recycling.

www.uk.freecycle.org
Freecycle – network of voluntary groups linking people who have things to get rid of with people who can use them.

www.foe.co.uk
Friends of the Earth – an environmental organisation that runs campaign on waste.

www.wastewatch.org.uk
Wastewatch – a national charity encouraging waste reduction, reuse and recycling.

www.wrap.org.uk
WRAP (Waste Resources Action Programme) – provides information to help business and consumers to be more efficient in their use of materials and recycle more waste. Their website has a special section for schools and communities.

Note to parents and teachers: Every effort has been made by the Publishers to ensure that these websites are suitable for children, that they are of the highest educational value, and that they contain no inappropriate or offensive material. However, because of the nature of the Internet, it is impossible to guarantee that the contents of these sites will not be altered. We strongly advise that Internet access is supervised by a responsible adult.

INDEX

These are the lists of contents for each title in *British Issues:*

Future Energy
The importance of energy • The state of energy today • Declining fossil fuels • Climate change • The nuclear debate • Wind power • Water power • Power from the Sun • Power from the Earth • Energy from waste • Innovations • Saving energy • Government and citizen action

Population Change
Britain's changing faces • Measuring change • People in the past • Population at work • Changing families • New lifestyles • Life moves • Trading places • Immigrants and emigrants • The European Union • Cultural identity • Ageing population • Looking to the future

Sporting Success
2012 • A rich history • Governing bodies •Funding • Facilities • Sport and society • The business of sport • Success stories • Sport and education • Fair play • Sport and the media • Sport and national pride • Looking towards 2012

Sustainable Cities
What does it mean to be a sustainable city? • Urban versus rural populations • Planning sustainable cities • Urban regeneration • Issues in the south-east • Stuck in the city • City movers • Sustainable energy • Water • Dealing with waste • Urban wildlife • Cities of opportunity • Vision of the future

Waste and Recycling
What is waste? • Throwaway society • What happens to waste? • Why waste matters • Managing waste • Reduce and reuse • Recycle! • How recycling happens • Composting • Energy from waste • Why don't we recycle more? • Changing the rules • A way to go

Water
Desert Britain? • The water industry • Water supply • Household water • Industry and agriculture • A growing gap • Climate change • The cost of water • Saving water • Drinking water • Water and the environment • Planning for the future • New technology